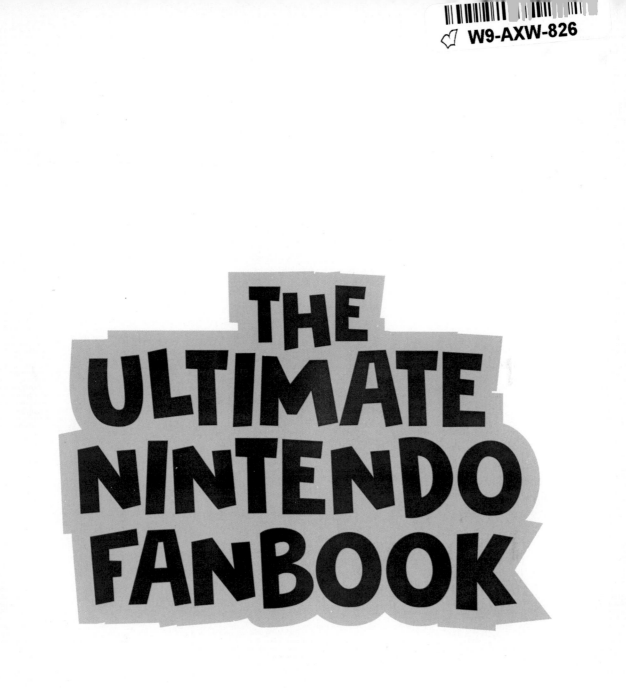

THE ULTIMATE NINTENDO FANBOOK

Published in 2022 by Mortimer Children's
An Imprint of Welbeck Children's Limited,
part of Welbeck Publishing Group
20 Mortimer Street, London W1T 3JW, UK
Based in London and Sydney.
www.welbeckpublishing.com

The publishers would like to thank the following sources for their kind permission to reproduce the pictures and footage in this book. The numbers listed below give the page on which they appear in the book.

Shutterstock (in order of appearance): 739photography 8/ robtek 12, 13/ Matthieu Tuffet 13/ David Peperkamp 19/ Tinxi 15/ Fit Ztudio 77

Gettyimages (in order of appearance): Sankei Archive 9

Every effort has been made to acknowledge correctly and contact the source and/or copyright holder of each picture. Any unintentional errors or omissions will be corrected in future editions.

ISBN 978 1 83935 214 0

Printed in Dongguan, China

10 9 8 7 6 5 4 3 2 1

Author: Kevin Pettman
Design: Darren Jordan and Rockjaw Creative, Ltd.
Design Manager: Sam James
Editorial Manager: Joff Brown
Production: Melanie Robertson

THE ULTIMATE NINTENDO FANBOOK

MORTIMER

CONTENTS

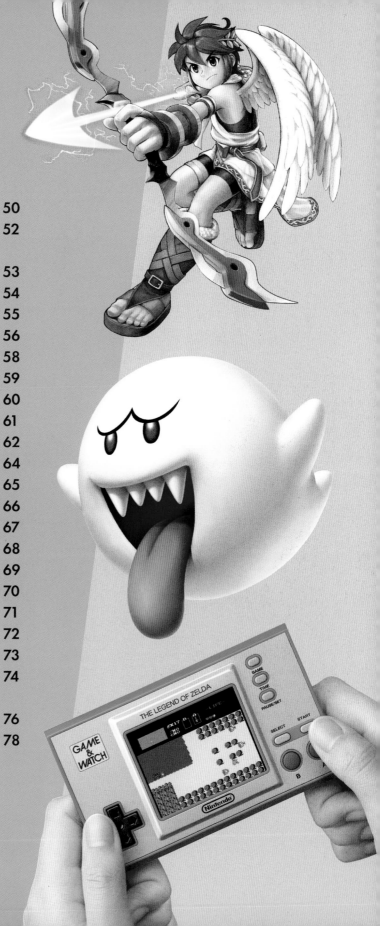

GREATEST GAMES

WE ♥ NINTENDO!

There's no bigger name in videogames than Nintendo—it has the coolest characters, consoles, games, and computer crazes! From Mario to Donkey Kong, Zelda to Pikachu, and with iconic machines such as the Switch, Game Boy, and Nintendo Entertainment System, the Japanese giants are total legends!

The Ultimate Nintendo Fanbook is your 100% unofficial guide to these gaming greats. It's packed with amazing info, fun facts, and secret stuff. Discover all about the record-breaking series *Super Mario Bros.*, *Mario Kart*, *Donkey Kong*, *Pokémon*, *The Legend of Zelda,* and loads more. See how Nintendo grew from making playing cards in the 1800s to leading the way with new consoles and videogame tech today. You can even take a glimpse into a fascinating future.

Let the action begin and enjoy your adventure through the greatest gaming galaxy!

PLAYING THE (CARD) GAME

See how Nintendo rose from simple card products to bossing the world of arcades and home console action!

Long before the creation of our favorite pixel-powered pals, Nintendo started making playing cards. The company was set up by craftsman Fusajiro Yamauchi in 1889 in the Japanese city of Kyoto. Yamauchi's flower-based "Hanafuda" cards were very popular and soon they were selling other playing cards around the world.

TOY STORY

The beautiful cards showed nature scenes, and the business also produced other picture cards from Japanese and western culture. These were big sellers until the 1960s, but by that time Hiroshi Yamauchi—Fusajiro's great grandson—was leading the company and had his eyes on children's toys. Nintendo was now making cards showing Disney characters, as well as other toy products. In the 1970s, children's electronic games and arcade equipment would really rocket Nintendo's fortunes!

EPIC ELECTRONICS

Nintendo's *Beam Gun* opto-electronic toys were a big hit in Japan in the early '70s. Using simple light technology, these fun shooters were very revolutionary. A laser clay shooting system and other arcade games were huge too. Home-use videogame technology was developed, leading to around a million sales each in Japan of the Color TV-Game 6 and TV-Game 15 systems—Nintendo's first gaming consoles!

GAMING FUTURE
The technology that Nintendo developed would help them go on to create the Famicom console— see page 12 for more.

DONKEY KONG COMES ALONG

Make way for the game-changing ape of the 1980s... and a name-changing hero!

The new generation of gamers were yelling out for a new screen hero—and not many yell louder than Donkey Kong! Nintendo artist Shigeru Miyamoto had the idea for a rampaging ape called Donkey Kong. This hairy horror was the star of an arcade game in 1981. Donkey Kong goes bananas, kidnaps Lady, and dashes to the top of a construction site. A super savior named Jumpman comes to her rescue. Ever heard of him?!

Donkey Kong and his family pop up in all kinds of games!

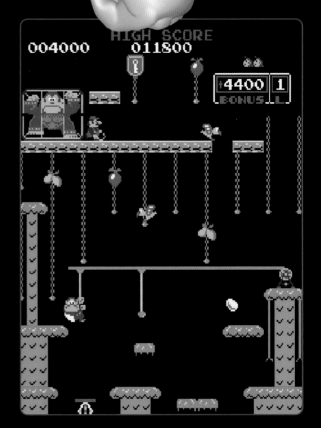

MARIO IS BORN

Jumpman was actually the original name given to Mario! In 1981 he was described as a carpenter (not the famous plumber we all know!) and he leaped into action to save Lady and beat barrel-bashing Donkey Kong. The arcade fun kept fans pumping in their coins as they tried to progress through the levels.

NAME GAME

Jumpman was a fans' fave in *Donkey Kong*. Nintendo wanted to make more use of him in the future, but his name was a bit boring! As Nintendo settled into their new US headquarters in New York at this time, they noticed that their mustached office landlord looked a bit like Jumpman. The landlord's name was Mario Segale, and the character was rebranded as Mario in his honour. A videogame star—and Nintendo's icon—was born!

D FOR DONKEY

Game & Watch *Donkey Kong* was the first time Nintendo used the directional pad (d-pad) control.

ANNIVERSARY EDITIONS

Nintendo released limited edition 35th anniversary Game & Watch versions of *Super Mario Bros.* and *The Legend of Zelda.*

WATCH OUT

There's no escaping that "DK" was Nintendo's breakout star in the early '80s. The Game & Watch portable LCD videogame devices were launched in Japan in 1980, with the *Donkey Kong* version in 1982 going on to reach a million sales worldwide. This was also the first time an existing Nintendo character starred in Game & Watch.

GAME & WATCH

THE LEGEND OF ZELDA

GAME
TIME
PAUSE/SET
SELECT
START
B
A

Nintendo

TIME TO ENTERTAIN

Home gaming goes up a gear as two awesome products make their mark—the NES and Game Boy!

One of the biggest moments in Nintendo's history was the release of the Nintendo Entertainment System. Better known as the NES, work on it began in Japan in 1983, with the console reaching US homes in 1985 and then Europe the following year. Boasting a sleek custom processing unit (CPU) and picture processing unit (PPU), the NES also used cartridges. This meant that, for the first time, a Nintendo console was capable of playing different titles. The company's variety of popular games and characters could be enjoyed on it once the NES was linked to a television.

FAMILY FUN
In Japan, the NES was originally branded as the Family Computer, or FamiCom for short.

The original NES was many kids' first experience of console gaming.

GAME RANGE

With US rival Atari struggling, the stage was set for Nintendo and the NES to dominate home gaming. *Donkey Kong* and *Donkey Kong Jr.* were successful NES games with others such as *Excitebike, Metroid, Punch-Out!, The Legend of Zelda,* and of course *Super Mario Bros.* all making their way to cartridges. By 1988 there were more than 60 games available for the millions of NES-loving fans!

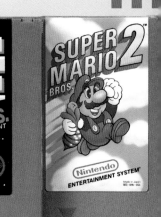

Nintendo Entertainment System

Years: 1983 to 1995 (2003 in Japan)

Sales: 62 million

Nintendo's range of titles excited early gaming fans.

PORTABLE POWER

The glorious Game Boy was yet another product that helped put Nintendo in control of the gaming universe! Unleashed in 1989, it was their first portable, handheld system and it also used game cartridges. Bundled with the addictive *Tetris* title, the Game Boy flew off the shelves, and with later Game Boy Color and Game Boy Advance versions, it's one of the biggest and best devices of all time.

Game Boy

Years: 1989 to 2003

Sales: 119 million (plus 81.5 million Game Boy Advance)

NINTENDO GOES SUPER

You've discovered the story of the NES and Game Boy, but did you know about these other cool Nintendo machines?

Super Nintendo Entertainment System

Years: 1990 to 2003
Sales: 49 million

Whether fans called it Super NES or SNES, this 16-bit system was a great follow-up to the top-selling NES. With superior graphics and sound, a better controller, and smash hit games such as *Super Mario World*, *Super Mario Kart*, and *Street Fighter II: The World Warrior*, SNES kept Nintendo fans very happy. If more gaming firepower was needed, the Score Master control pad and joystick did the business!

Nintendo 64

Years: 1996 to 2003
Sales: 33 million

With its clever controller and powerful 64-bit tech, the Nintendo 64 was a striking addition to Nintendo's console range. Graphics looked 3D instead of flat, four players could connect to it, and over 500,000 were sold on the first day alone! A groundbreaking new accessory from Nintendo was the Rumble Pak attachment to the N64 controller. Players got a shuddering sensation when something big happened on screen.

Games like the **Tony Hawk's Pro Skater** series used the N64's 3D graphics to make (sort of) realistic-looking environments!

NEW N64 TITLES
Pilotwings 64, *Super Mario 64*, and *Star Fox 64* were games that helped launch the N64 console.

Nintendo GameCube

Years: 2001 to 2009
Sales: 22 million

Nintendo changed the shape of videogame consoles in 2001 with the GameCube. This boxy system looked very different from the sleeker N64 and SNES. Perhaps the GameCube's biggest impact was the WaveBird. It was a wireless controller and was named because it used radio "waves". Without a cable, players were then free to wander like a "bird" when playing!

The chaotic karting adventures continued as new technology developed.

Nintendo Wii

Years: 2006 to 2017
Sales: 101 million

The Wii pulled in millions of new Nintendo gamers! People who hadn't enjoyed videogames before were now hooked with this all-action system, especially the hugely successful *Wii Sports* game. With the wireless motion sensor Wii Remote Plus, a sensor bar, and optional Nunchuk remote, Nintendo Wii was great fun with friends, family, and for solo play. *Mario Kart Wii*, *Wii Fit* and *Super Smash Bros. Brawl* all helped the console smash 100 million sales!

Wii remotes were available in different colours and themes—like this Luigi design!

Despite lower sales, the Wii U was still a classic console.

Wii U

Years: 2012 to 2017
Sales: 13 million

Despite having the lowest console sales (apart from the early Color TV-Game) in Nintendo's history, the Wii U was still a great piece of gear with excellent features. The high definition system's big attraction was the GamePad controller. It had a 6.2-inch touch screen and Nintendo bragged it was a "second window into the videogame world." Nintendo also created the online Miiverse for users to share experiences and chat about games.

Master the Miiverse on the Wii U!

Wii Mini

Years: 2012 to 2017
Sales: No data

Cashing in on the Wii's mega success, Wii Mini was a smaller and cheaper version. Just like the original it came with a Wii Remote Plus and Nunchuk, and could also hook up with fun accessories like the Wheel and Balance Board for crazy gaming fun. Access to the Nintendo Selects games, including *Wii Sports Resorts* and *Mario Party 8*, boosted its popularity.

Nintendo Switch

Years: 2017 to now
Sales: 103 million

Along with the NES and Game Boy, Nintendo Switch is a system that's ripped up the gaming industry! Acting as both a console and a handheld, the Switch offers amazing versatility as a touchscreen tablet that can dock and link to a TV screen. The new dual Joy-Con lets two players get in on the action, or the controllers can attach either side of the Switch and be played in your hands just like a traditional setup.

SWITCH UP

By the end of 2021, there were over 100 million Switch sales and it became Nintendo's greatest home console within just five years!

Triple fun

With three ways to play—in TV mode with the Joy-Con grip, tabletop sharing, or handheld—Nintendo Switch became the ultimate way for individuals and groups to get the most from a home system. The Switch Lite arrived in 2019 as a smaller and more affordable version and its only real limitation was not being able to dock and connect to a TV. Playing *Mario Kart 8 Deluxe* on the Switch never loses its appeal!

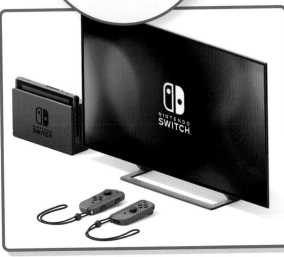

HANDHELD HEROES!

Nintendo has put so much fun and action at your fingertips over the years. Check out some of the ultimate handheld heroes.

Meet the master of Nintendo handhelds—the DS! This legendary item has been bought by over 150 million gamers. Back in 2004 its dual-screen touch tech was a game changer, and games could be displayed on one or both of the screens. Coming with a stylus, the DS allowed you to draw pictures and control functions with ease, plus the WiFi connection linked users with others around the world.

Play with your heroes while on the move? Yes please, Pikachu!

READY TO RUMBLE

Some Nintendo DS games, such as *Actionloop* and *Metroid Prime Pinball*, were enhanced with the DS Rumble Pak accessory.

Nintendo DS

Years: 2004 to 2015

Sales: 154 million

FAB FOLLOW-UPS

The DS was super popular and was followed by the DS Lite, DSi, and DSi XL. The DSi came with two built-in cameras, meaning owners could take fun photos and share them. Just like the original DS, it also had a DS Activity Meters option which could track the distance you walked and your movement patterns. This technology was literally going places!

MORE MOBILE DEVICES

Nintendo has a rich history of handheld successes. The Game Boy Advance served epic releases like *Pokémon Ruby and Sapphire* and *Pokémon FireRed and LeafGreen*. The 3DS came along in 2011 and would eventually reach 75 million sales and give Nintendo the power to project heroes like Zelda, Kirby, and Mario in fascinating 3D function!

STRANGE STUFF

Even with millions of sales and billions in the bank, Nintendo and its partners also had some wacky ideas! Virtual Boy (1995) was a weird visor that hoped to capture 3D gaming, but the console failed within a year. In 1989 the wearable Power Glove was designed to take action games in a new direction—nice idea, but the tech didn't work well. Other failed ventures include the R.O.B. (Robotic Operating Body) in 1985, the floor mat Power Pad (1986), and the Game Boy Camera and Printer (1998). These items are rare gems these days!

Ninendo's handheld consoles take the Game Boy's legacy to new heights.

Fans young and old snapped up millions of DS devices, titles and accessories.

NINTENDO SUPERSTARS

It's time to get up close with all of the biggest Nintendo characters! This bunch of videogame legends have starred on our screens for decades and with their superpowers, skills and charm, they keep on entertaining us. Get ready for a trip through the Nintendo hall of fame...

MARIO

First appearance: *Donkey Kong* (arcade game)

Debut year: 1981

Likes: Mushrooms

Dislikes: Bowser

Not only is Mario the most recognisable Nintendo character, he's also the biggest videogame star ever! From leaping around, collecting coins, and jumping down pipes to saving Princess Peach, cruising in karts, and globe-trotting hat-powered adventures, Mario has been the main man for over 40 years.

MARIO MOVES

Super Mario Bros. was the first game to bring all of the classic Mario things together. Since the 1980s, the plucky plumber has moved from basic 2D action and battles with Bowser to 3D thrills in *Super Mario 64* (1996), space encounters on the Wii with *Super Mario Galaxy* (2007), to fighting with Inklings and Pikachu in *Super Smash Bros. Ultimate* (2018). Every time Mario faces a fresh challenge, his bravery and determination to eliminate evil always saves the day!

Dashing, jumping, driving, building, fighting... Mario can do it all!

HISTORY MAKER

The Mario series of videogames have recorded over 770 million sales, making it the biggest franchise in gaming history.

Mario's levels are filled with challenges... it's especially fun when you make your own!

TOP JOB

He's the most popular plumber ever, but Mario has done stacks of jobs in his five decades of popping up in awesome Nintendo games. His first medical shift was in *Doctor Mario* in the 1990s, followed by being a tennis ace in *Mario's Tennis* and other sporting roles such as *Mario Superstar Baseball,* and a gold medal hero in *Mario & Sonic at the Olympic Games. Mario Paint* made him an artist and his builder skills were displayed in *Super Mario Maker!*

LEGENDARY LIKES

To be a true Mario fan, you need to know what really makes this cool character tick and what his likes are! Obviously his brother is the legendary Luigi, he loves gobbling and grabbing mushrooms, and his closest friends include Princess Peach, Princess Daisy, Yoshi, and Toad. He's also fond of mustaches and meatballs!

Mario Kart World Tour on smartphones is a speed spectacular!

LUIGI

First appearance: *Mario Bros.*
Debut year: 1983
Likes: Vacuuming ghosts
Dislikes: Waluigi

Luigi's always ready to face his biggest fears!

Looking much like his brother, Luigi is not as brave as Mario but is always willing to be part of the team and keep the Mushroom Kingdom safe. Nintendo finally put him center stage in 2013 for his 30th anniversary, declaring it the "Year of Luigi" with the excellent adventures of *Luigi's Mansion 2, New Super Luigi 2, Mario & Luigi: Dream Team,* and *Dr. Luigi.* Nice work, bro!

DONKEY KONG

First appearance:
Donkey Kong (arcade game)
Debut year: 1981
Likes: Bananas
Dislikes: King K. Rool

Feed him the yellow stuff and he's happy!

After his arcade success, *Donkey Kong* came to the NES in 1983 in Japan. He has since developed from being Mario's rival to more of a goofy and well-natured sidekick. With great strength and a menacing look, he reached hero status in *Donkey Kong Country* on the SNES (1994) and regularly features with Nintendo's other big stars. DK is a totally great ape!

PRINCESS PEACH

First appearance:
Super Mario Bros.

Debut year: 1985

Likes: Pink things

Dislikes: Being kidnapped

Peach is just at home on the race track as in the palace!

You'd think after all this time, Princess Peach would now be wise to constantly being taken by Bowser and instead would just live a quiet life in the Princess Peach Castle! With Mario, Luigi, Toad, and the gang helping her, this Mushroom Kingdom royalty has survived many scrapes in countless games. In *Super Princess Peach* (2006) the roles reversed and she got to rescue Mario!

Super cute and super loyal. Respect to the Toad!

TOAD

First appearance:
Super Mario Bros.

Debut year: 1985

Likes: Protecting Princess Peach

Dislikes: Letting people down

One of the most loyal and likeable characters in the Mushroom Kingdom, Toad does his best to keep everyone happy and battle evil forces. What he lacks in strength and size he makes up for with speed, which makes an interesting mix in the *Mario Kart* series. *Captain Toad: Treasure Tracker* (2014) is the only time the Toads have had a starring title role, though!

YOSHI

First appearance:
Super Mario World

Debut year: 1990

Likes: Flutter jumps

Dislikes: Having no cookies

Mario is forever delighted that he cracked open Yoshi's egg and that the pair became great pals! The friendly green dinosaur has a slick set of game-winning skills, including his long and powerful tongue and accurate egg throwing. Titles like *Yoshi's Crafted World*, *Yoshi's New Island* and the puzzle-based classic *Yoshi's Cookie* have kept the cool character on our screens.

The greatest dino in the Nintendo world, Yoshi is always ready to help Mario and Luigi.

DINOSAUR DETAIL
Did you know that Yoshi's full name is actually T. Yoshisaur Munchakoopas? Yoshi is much easier to say and remember!

WARIO

First appearance:
Super Mario Land 2: Golden Coins

Debut year: 1992

Likes: Being greedy

Dislikes: Mario

First showing up on the Game Boy in the early 1990s, Wario is often seen as Mario's evil counterpart. The 'W' on his cap could easily stand for wicked rather than his name! Wario's classic pose of clenched fists and nasty grin is something Nintendo fans have seen so often over 30-plus years...he's a gruesome guy but for some reason never stops thinking he's hugely handsome!

Beware the evil deeds of the wicked Wario!

WALUIGI

First appearance: *Mario Tennis*

Debut year: 2000

Likes: Tennis

Dislikes: Being nice

Put on the purple and become a master of mayhem with Waluigi!

If you've played tennis on a Nintendo then you'll have no doubt come up against the evil Waluigi. Created to give Luigi a direct opponent in the same way Wario does to Mario, Waluigi arrived in *Mario Tennis* and then in many other tennis-themed games afterward. He's a sneaky character that you should never trust in a sporting arena or anywhere else!

Bowser and his evil family are always making nasty plans!

BOWSER

First appearance:
Super Mario Bros.

Debut year: 1985

Likes: Kidnapping

Dislikes: Not ruling the Mushroom Kingdom

Bowser is perhaps the biggest and baddest videogame enemy ever created! As the King of the Koopas, he rules his family and threatens the Mushroom Kingdom with an iron claw. His offspring are Bowser Jr., Larry, Iggy, Wendy O. Koopa, Lemmy, Roy, Morton Jr., and Ludwig Von Koopa. Together they create havoc for Mario and the rest of the Nintendo good guys!

ROSALINA

First appearance: *Super Mario Galaxy*

Debut year: 2007

Likes: Lumas

Dislikes: Unfriendly galaxies

The mysterious and magical Rosalina adopts the look of Princess Peach and Daisy, but this intergalactic force likes to operate in a star-studded universe. She's most at home high up in the galaxy and as the mother figure to the Luma characters she's kind, caring, and protective. Rosalina has appeared in series such as *Super Mario 3D World, Mario Kart,* and *Super Smash Bros.*

Become a big star as the royal-looking Rosalina.

GOOMBA

First appearance: *Super Mario Bros.*

Debut year: 1985

Likes: Fungus

Dislikes: Being stomped on

A group of troublesome Goombas is a common sight in the Nintendo universe. Having been featured in hundreds of games and spinoffs, Goombas may be weak but they possess strength in numbers. Before they joined Bowser's Koopa Troop they were actually a peace-loving collection of small brown mushroomlike creatures. Maybe they'll go back to being good one day!

KOOPA TROOPA

First appearance: *Super Mario Bros.*

Debut year: 1985

Likes: Being in the Koopa Troop

Dislikes: Retreating into their shell

SHELL SHOCKED

In the 1983 *Mario Bros.* arcade game, shellcreepers were Nintendo's first turtle-powered enemies.

Look out for these colorful menaces making a scene, causing obstructions, and firing their super shells during hundreds of Nintendo adventures. Common in green, yellow, blue, and red, these pesky turtlelike dudes are often loyal to Bowser but be prepared for them to carry out their own battle agendas. Koopa Troopas can be turtle-y annoying at times!

Expect the unexpected with the Koopa Troopa dudes!

PIRANHA PLANT

First appearance: *Super Mario Bros.*

Debut year: 1985

Likes: Chomping and eating

Dislikes: Being hungry

Are piranha plants real Nintendo characters or just background features? Well, they pop up all over the place and this fearsome fauna will take a bite out of you at every opportunity, so they deserve your attention! Piranha Plants are classic Mario enemies that originally hid in pipes but will now attack from lots of places. Stay away from the pinching plants!

Watch out for surprise attacks from this pain-dealing plant!

29

PRINCESS DAISY

First appearance: *Super Mario Land*

Debut year: 1989

Likes: Luigi

Dislikes: Losing

Don't be fooled by the cute clothes and appearance, because Princess Daisy has a feisty streak to rival many Nintendo heroes! With a history going back to the 1980s, Daisy has come a long way since being rescued by Mario, and with her debut as an echo fighter in *Super Smash Bros. Ultimate* (2018) fans really got to see her power-packed abilities!

Keep the Princess on your side, because she's a powerful character!

BIRDO

First appearance:
Doki Doki Panic

Debut year: 1987

Likes: Yoshi

Dislikes: Not being on screen

Birdo arrived in the Japanese *Doki Doki Panic* game as a boss character and the dino's popularity has grown over the years. Often seen as a match-up for Yoshi, the eye-catching prehistoric pink creation has been let lose in games such as *Super Mario Party* and *Mario Tennis* on the N64. Birdo should really be a bigger part of more games and a regular on our computer screens!

Is it time for Birdo to fly high as a title character?

CAPPY

First appearance: *Super Mario Odyssey*

Debut year: 2017

Likes: Being thrown

Dislikes: Bowser

When his little sister Tiara is taken by Bowser in the Cap Kingdom, Cappy teams up with Mario to set about saving her. He's a popular new character and with the ability to defeat enemies, possess them, or even transport Mario, Cappy's hat-powered skills are head and shoulders above the evil folk he and Mario face. Cappy is *heading* for big things!

Keep hold of your hat... Cappy always makes a headline appearance!

BOWSER JR.

First appearance: *Super Mario Sunshine*

Debut year: 2002

Likes: Koopa Clown Car

Dislikes: Getting his bib dirty

As the next in line to the Bowser throne, little Bowser Jr. has much to live up to in the Nintendo world! In *Mario & Rabbids: Kingdom Battle* he attempts to take over the Mushroom Kingdom and throughout his devilish gaming career, Bowser Jr. has shown a smart but sneaky side that suggests he'd be a better leader if dad ever stepped aside!

Like father, like son? Bowser Jr. can be a smart enemy!

BOOM BOOM

First appearance:
Super Mario Bros. 3

Debut year: 1988

Likes: Koopalings

Dislikes: Stomp attacks

A spiky character with a lot of influence in Bowser's Koopa Troop, Boom Boom brings the battle every time he's unleashed in the Mushroom Kingdom! His sharp teeth give him real bite up against Mario and Luigi and with high jumps, spinning arm attacks, and flaming trails Boom Boom has been a fierce force since the 1980s.

Are you brave enough to bite back against Boom Boom?

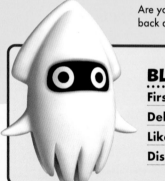

BLOOPER

First appearance: *Super Mario Bros.*

Debut year: 1985

Likes: Oceans

Dislikes: Ink shortage

A scary squidlike species which can be dangerous on land as well as in water, Bloopers are guided by the boss Gooper Blooper. They can launch nasty ink attacks and their tentacles will tie opponents up in trouble. Bloopers vary in size and ferociousness depending on the game they're in—*Mario Party 8* was the first time they became a playable character.

'Ink' carefully before taking on the Bloopers!

In case you didn't know, it's always hammer time with these characters!

HAMMER BRO.

First appearance: *Super Mario Bros.*

Debut year: 1985

Likes: Hammers

Dislikes: *Mario Kart* crowds

From the Koopa species, Hammer Bros. have the power to throw hammers and with large shells and helmets they always stand out in a crowd of baddies. Talking of crowds, Hammer Bros. have appeared in several *Mario Kart* games but just in the crowd or as background characters—it's about time these creations actually got behind the wheel!

HOT STUFF

Fire Bros. are a rarer variety of the Hammer Bros. with red shells and helmet.

BULLET BILL

First appearance: *Super Mario Bros.*

Debut year: 1985

Likes: Blasting off

Dislikes: Not hitting their target

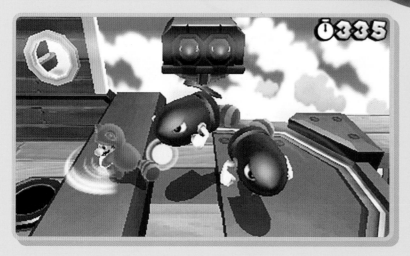

Zooming out from a bill blaster canon is when Bullet Bills cause maximum damage. Stacks of games have seen this epic ammo unleashed and whether in flaming red, gold, or any other color, they have just one mission...to reach their target! Once these crazy characters have been fired, Mario and the gang must react or take the hit.

Keep a close eye on these pesky foes during your Nintendo adventures.

SHY GUY

First appearance: *Doki Doki Panic*

Debut year: 1987

Likes: Being shy

Dislikes: Taking off the mask

With five decades of Nintendo appearances on their record, Shy Guys are unmistakable characters, particularly in the *Mario Party* and *Mario Kart* series. The little dudes may come across as friendly at times and perhaps as just a walking nuisance, however the brightly-colored enemies have a pesky presence that makes up for their small stature. Beware of their quiet ways!

What mischief lurks behind those memorable masks?

Less dangerous than they look, Boos can still freak you out!

BOO

First appearance: *Super Mario Bros. 3*

Debut year: 1988

Likes: Hiding in the dark

Dislikes: Vacuum cleaners

Tongues hanging out, jagged teeth, ghostly expressions...Boos are a sight to behold! Luckily, their appearance is generally worse than any damage they can inflict. If they spring a surprise from a hideout in a dark and spooky place, staring at them results in Boos freezing still and then covering their eyes. Their in-built shyness really reduces their attack powers!

DIDDY KONG

First appearance: *Donkey Kong Country*

Debut year: 1994

Likes: Swinging and jumping

Dislikes: Losing bananas

LOVE INTEREST

Diddy Kong's girlfriend is Dixie Kong. She debuted in *Donkey Kong Country 2: Diddy's Kong Quest.*

If there's one character that Donkey Kong trusts, it's his best friend and nephew Diddy Kong. He's not as brawny as his big buddy, but Diddy's strengths are his speed, agility, and jumping which makes him a great partner for DK on Donkey Kong Island. With his red cap and yellow-starred shirt, Diddy Kong is another great Nintendo ape!

Diddy Kong and his bigger uncle make a strong duo!

BOB-OMB

First appearance: *Super Mario Bros. 2*

Debut year: 1986

Likes: Explosions

Dislikes: Short fuses

Found throughout the Mushroom Kingdom, Bob-ombs enjoy making an explosive entry! With the skill to move and with eyes and a wind-up key, Bob-ombs need to be handled with care and kept at a safe distance if possible. Racing fans will remember them showing up in *Mario Kart: Double Dash* (2003) and being chucked by Wario and Waluigi to cause chaos in a race!

Stand back and take cover from these round rascals!

PIKACHU

First appearance: *Pokémon Red* and *Blue*

Debut year: 1996 (Japan)

Likes: Electricity

Dislikes: Losing in *Super Smash Bros.*

Pokémon are wild creatures that come in all shapes and sizes, but the most famous shape and size is definitely Pikachu! Older than many Mario game-based characters, the electric-type Pokémon is so highly charged and powerful that Nintendo couldn't contain it to just this series. In 1999, Pikachu also became a starter in the original *Super Smash Bros.* title!

Pikachu is always happy to make an electrifying appearance!

JIGGLYPUFF

First appearance:
Pokémon Red and *Blue*

Debut year: 1996 (Japan)

Likes: Singing you to sleep

Dislikes: Being small

Another *Pokémon* world star, Jigglypuff comes from the balloon species and will inflate itself if angered! It evolved from Igglybuff and with big round eyes, a distinctive curl, and cute pink features, Jigglypuff will happily lull you into a false sense of security. It may look like a marshmallow and softer than a swimming pool of cushions, but it's a tough fighter when the pressure's on!

Cute and cuddly? Don't be fooled by Jigglypuff!

CHARIZARD

First appearance:
Pokémon Red and *Blue*

Debut year: 1996 (Japan)

Likes: Fire

Dislikes: Weak opponents

Any *Pokémon* trainer would love to be in charge of Charizard! Watch out for the tip of its tail burning bright as it spits hot flames and circles high in the sky. As fearsome and fire-fueled as they are, Charizards are also rather noble and don't seek out weaker rivals. They instead prefer to match up with their equals and deploy their dragon dynamism on worthy opponents!

Charizard is a well respected character and a brave competitor.

MEWTWO

First appearance:
Pokémon Red and *Blue*

Debut year: 1996 (Japan)

Likes: Aggression

Dislikes: Speaking or smiling

Legendary psychic *Pokémon* Mewtwo has been described as a cross between a cat and a squirrel, but whatever you think of it, this creation is capable of battling the very best. Scientifically forged from the genes of Mew, this two-legged beast shows little mercy and thanks to its savage mind and strength, it takes some stopping. Good luck with that!

Never rest with Mewtwo on the scene.

ZACIAN

First appearance:
Pokémon Sword and *Shield*

Debut year: 2019

Likes: Swords

Dislikes: Battle injuries

Warriors are super cool in the *Pokémon* universe, showing off an air of power, ruthlessness, and respect. Zacian is a wolflike creature that already has a big fanbase even though it only appeared in 2019. When holding its weapon in its mouth it changes to crowned sword form—super, super cool!

Keep a safe distance from the battle-ready Zacian.

ROWLET

First appearance:
Pokémon Sun and Moon

Debut year: 2016

Likes: Kicking

Dislikes: Being light

One of three new starter *Pokémon* in the seventh generation of games, alongside Litten and Popplio, Rowlet is something of a dark threat. It uses photosynthesis to harness power during the day, ready to unleash it when night falls. Rowlet's silent gliding, sharp feathers, and excellent night vision make it much more powerful than its appearance would suggest!

Rowlet enjoys a special set of game-changing skills.

Sleep easy, Snorlax!

SNORLAX

First appearance:
Pokémon Red and *Blue*

Debut year: 1996 (Japan)

Likes: Eating and sleeping

Dislikes: Belly being bounced on

Not every *Pokémon* hero is an all action, energetic fighter that constantly wants to be in the spotlight. Snorlax likes nothing better than resting and dozing before waking when it's ready to fill its face with food. Nice life, hey? Just be careful not to wake a sleeping Snorlax and then risk changing it into a grumpy and dangerous attacker!

EEVEE

First appearance:
Pokémon Red and *Blue*

Debut year: 1996 (Japan)

Likes: Evolving

Dislikes: Looking like Pikachu

As proof of how popular Eevee is, *Pokémon: Let's Go, Eevee!* made the character a Nintendo title star in 2018! Eevee's well known for having an irregular genetic code, meaning it has the potential to evolve into one of eight other forms. This impressive ability, mixed with a cute and friendly look, marks the creature out as one to back in any situation.

Eevee comes in a variety of forms, so always be on guard.

LINK

First appearance: *The Legend of Zelda*

Debut year: 1986

Likes: Fighting

Dislikes: Not fighting

The hero of Hyrule, Link has been seen at various ages throughout the Zelda franchise but one thing stays the same—his quest to protect the princess and the land, and outsmart Ganon and the villains. He takes a title role in *Link's Awakening, A Link Between Worlds, A Link to the Past,* and *The Adventure of Link,* plus some mighty moves against Cia in *Hyrule Warriors*!

MASTER MARIO

Look out for Link revving up his speedy master cycle zero motorbike in 2014's *Mario Kart 8*!

Link never backs away from a battle with Ganon.

PRINCESS ZELDA

First appearance: *The Legend of Zelda*

Debut year: 1986

Likes: Link

Dislikes: Ganon

Nintendo states that Princess Zelda is "wise beyond her years" thanks to her knowledge of the Triforce of Wisdom. Zelda's royal status in the medieval kingdom of Hyrule gives her great power but she's always under constant threat from the evil Ganon. Her skills with a bow, magical mind, and loyalty to the kingdom make her a difficult character to defeat!

A powerful and iconic character, Zelda is a true Nintendo hero.

GANON

First appearance:
The Legend of Zelda

Debut year: 1986

Likes: Evil

Dislikes: Link

What's the difference between Ganondorf and Ganon in *The Legend of Zelda*? Ganon is the beastly incarnation of Ganondorf once the transformation powers of the Triforce take place. Looking like a boar but with the power and prowess of a mythical god, this evil opponent pushes Link and Zelda to the edge in every game they contest.

With a fearsome look and mighty powers, Ganon deserves total respect.

IMPA

First appearance: *The Legend of Zelda*

Debut year: 1986

Likes: Protecting Princess Zelda

Dislikes: The monstrous Demise

Zelda fans will know that Impa popped up in the manual for the NES's The Legend of Zelda, before later becoming a mainstay in the fantasy fighting franchise. She comes from the Sheikah tribe and loves nothing better than teaming up with Link as a guardian of Zelda and stopping Ganon in his tracks. Older than she looks, Impa has a valuable knowledge of the Hyrule kingdom.

Link and Zelda are lucky to call on Impa's knowledge!

KIRBY

First appearance: *Kirby's Dream Land*

Debut year: 1992

Likes: Sucking in

Dislikes: Boss enemies

Small, round, and very pink, Kirby has the unique power to suck in and absorb enemies and objects and copy their abilities. He lives in Dream Land, on the planet Pop Star, and in the Kirby series he's constantly battling King Dede and Meta Knight, usually with help from Waddle Dees. This may seem a bit weird, but once you're in control of Kirby the fun and action are non-stop!

Kirby has a strange way of beating enemies, but his skills are impressive!

KIRBY COUNT

Kirby is the title hero in over 30 games. The first on Switch was 2018's *Kirby Star Allies*.

KING DEDE

First appearance: *Kirby's Dream Land*

Debut year: 1992

Likes: Giant hammer

Dislikes: Kirby...or does he?

King Dede thinks he's the ruler of Dream Land, but really the country's folks don't take much notice of the trouble-making character! Nintendo reckons he is Kirby's "arch frenemy" as although the pair squabble they may also team up for the good of the nation alongside Meta Knight. With his huge wooden hammer King Dede likes to have a smashing time on screen!

King of Dream Land or just a nuisance? You decide!

SAMUS ARAN

First appearance: *Metroid*

Debut year: 1986

Likes: Intergalactic bounty hunting

Dislikes: Metroids

If you don't know much about the heroic space hunter Samus Aran then it's about time you do! As a historic Nintendo character from the awesome *Metroid* series, she has a huge army of fans who love her intergalactic fighting powers and the determination she has to defeat Space Pirates and Metroid creatures. Samus is a sci-fi superstar!

The hunt is trully on when Samus Aran sets her sights on the target.

SONIC

First appearance: *Sonic Adventure 2: Battle*

Debut year: 2001

Likes: Speed

Dislikes: Dr. Robotnik

When Sega stopped making consoles, the speedy Sonic arrived on Nintendo devices and made his debut in *Sonic Adventure 2: Battle*. He's now known for teaming up with Mario and the gang in slick Olympics sports games, in the *Super Smash Bros.* series, and in hits like *Sonic Mania* and *Sonic Colors: Ultimate*. He became a Nintendo star in super-fast time!

Sonic raced into Nintendo stardom!

RYU

First appearance: *Street Fighter II: The World Warrior*

Debut year: 1992

Likes: Hadouken

Dislikes: Losing

Street Fighter was a mega arcade hit in the 1980s and the game first came to the SNES in 1992. Ryu is an all-around Japanese martial arts hero and will deploy his special hadouken fireball to punish his opponents. He has a friendly rivalry with Ken but as a traditional tough guy he takes losing very, very badly!

DANGEROUS DRIVE
....
Ryu became DLC (downloadable content) as a car racer in the cool *Hot Wheels* Unleashed Switch game in 2022.

The contest kicks off when these fighters use their masterful moves!

KEN MASTERS

First appearance:
Street Fighter II: The World Warrior

Debut year: 1992

Likes: Shoryuken

Dislikes: Losing

Ryu's long-term friendly foe, when Ken unleashes his special shoryuken uppercut move it can be a game changer. The US fighter wears his iconic red suit and as a martial arts "master" it takes a lot for Chun-Li, M. Bison, or any other classic character to put him down. In 2017's *Ultra Street Fighter II: The Final Challengers*, Violent Ken and Evil Ryu make dramatic appearances!

Ken never fails to master the battle arena!

ISABELLE

First appearance:
Animal Crossing: New Leaf

Debut year: 2012

Likes: Being friendly

Dislikes: Confrontation

The fun sim series *Animal Crossing* kicked off in 2001 and it took a little time for Isabelle to enter this world of cute pets and laid-back laughs. Now, though, she's the mascot of the popular franchise and is a friendly and helpful assistant to everyone she meets. This lovable dog is "always getting her paws dirty with town business" according to Nintendo, so never be afraid to seek her out!

The helpful hero in the Animal Crossing adventures.

RABBIDS

First appearance: *Rayman Raving Rabbids*

Debut year: 2006

Likes: Silly screaming

Dislikes: Bwario & Bwaluigi

It's rapid fun when the Rabbids are on your screen!

Nintendo has been a home for hundreds of crazy characters and Rabbids were another awesome addition in 2006! The world was introduced to the bonkers bunnies and their wacky ways and these days they have entered the Mushroom Kingdom with *Mario & Rabbids: Kingdom Battle* and *Mario & Rabbids: Sparks of Hope*. Rabbid Mario is a mega mashup character!

FOX McCLOUD

First appearance: *Star Fox*

Debut year: 1993

Likes: Leading his squadron

Dislikes: Andross

Brave pilot and fighter Fox McCloud mixes his aviation abilities with a fierce resolve to hunt down the villainous Andross and rid the Lylat System of evil! *Star Fox* sees McCloud and crew members Peppy Hare, Slippy Toad, and Falco Lombardi patrol the skies in their favorite Arwing spaceship and harness their creature powers for the good of the galaxy.

Fox McCloud has awesome flying and fighting skills!

GAME NAME

Pac-Man was originally going to be called Puck-Man before Namco, the game developers, changed the hero's name.

Watch out for ghastly ghosts in Pac-Man's games!

PAC-MAN

First appearance:
Pac-Land

Debut year: 1985

Likes: Munching

Dislikes: Ghosts

From a classic Namco arcade adventure that made its way onto consoles, Pac-Man is the dot-munching, maze-weaving hero with a terrible fear of ghosts Blinky, Pinky, Inky, and Clyde. *Pac-Man Party* on the Wii developed new mini-games and challenges for the yellow dude and 2022's *Pac-Man Museum* bundles 14 retro titles from the last 40 years. That mean it's time to get gobbling!

INKLING

First appearance: *Splatoon*

Debut year: 2015

Likes: Turf War

Dislikes: Octarians

These transforming humanoids will flip from kid to squid in an instant—the nickname "squid kids" really fits! The brightly-colored combatants enjoy firing ink from weapons like paintbrushes, rollers, and guns and then in squid form disguise themselves in the splats to hijack opponents. Clever, cunning, and not afraid to spray and play in Inkopolis!

Splatoon is packed with craziness and colour.

OCTARIAN

First appearance: Splatoon

Debut year: 2015

Likes: Shields and bombs

Dislikes: Inklings

Another humanoid group, this species will morph into octopus to get the upper hand over the Inklings! They like stealing electric-producing zapfish and with the guidance of DJ Octavio they make a formidable attack army. Octarians come in many different forms, including Octobomber and Octoling, but one thing that unites them is their determination to be bad!

Prepare for splat attacks and a messy scene on screen with these guys!

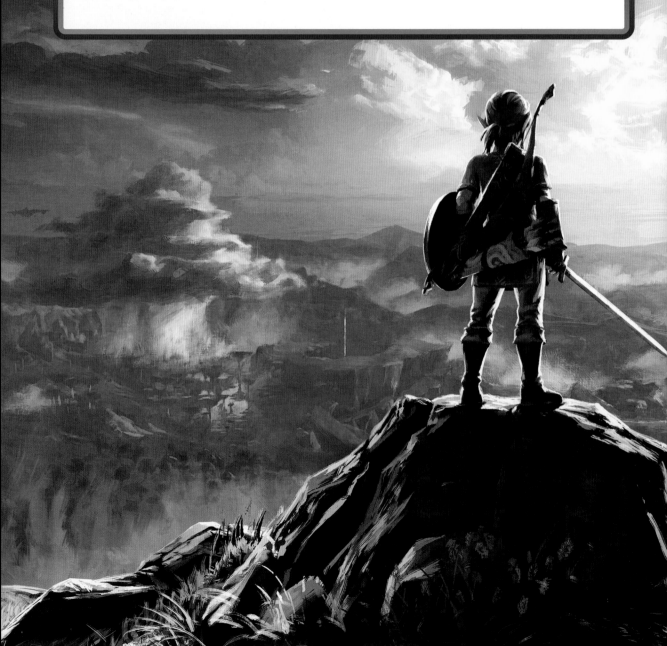

GREATEST GAMES

Grab your controller and lock your eyes on the screen because you're about to experience the greatest games in Nintendo history! From the world and wonders of **Super Mario Bros**. to **The Legend of Zelda**, **Pokémon**, **Splatoon**, the classic **Tetris,** and many more, these awesome videogames reveal everything you love about gaming. Enjoy the action!

SUPER MARIO BROS.

In the most famous series of Nintendo games, Mario teams up with Luigi, takes on Bowser, comes to Peach's rescue, and encounters a few mushrooms, plants, coins, and pipes...legendary *Super Mario Bros.* stuff!

The original *Super Mario Bros.* (1985) on the NES sees Mario dashing to avoid Bowser and his enemies, grab coins, storm castles, and seek out the Princess. Mushrooms make him Super Mario and fire flowers let him shoot fireballs! *Super Mario Bros. 2* was not so great, but *Super Mario Bros. 3* saw Mario's raccoon suit for the first time, plus the crazy Koopalings!

NEW ARRIVAL

New Super Mario Bros. (2006) was a smash success on the DS, with a new look that still had a cool retro style. *New Super Mario Bros. U* (2012) was Mario's first Wii U adventure and had new modes and features such as challenge mode and coin battle. *New Super Mario Bros. U Deluxe* (2019) brings the awesome series to the Switch, with the *New Super Luigi U* game giving the green guy a starring role in a platform adventure for the first time!

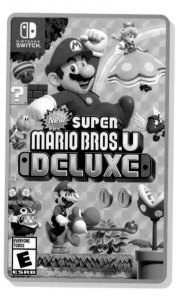

Mario and Luigi are joined by their biggest and best gaming friends.

SUPER MARIO BROS.

TOP TIP!

In *New Super Mario Bros. U Deluxe*, Nabbit and Toadette are new playable characters who are good for new and younger gamers. Nabbit doesn't suffer damage from enemies and Toadette's super crown power-up turns her into a Peachette. She can then double jump and float in freefall!

SECRET

Some *New Super Mario Bros. U Deluxe* courses have a secret exit, marked by a red goal pole flag. These special exits will reveal a secret path to take!

TOP TIP!

When two or more players time their jumps correctly, they can perform a synchro ground-pound and smash their bottoms down at the same time. It's a move that wipes out all grounded enemies you can see at that time in *New Super Mario Bros. U Deluxe!*

Keep playing to learn the best moves and tactics.

SUPER MARIO 3D WORLD

With Peach available as a playable character, alongside Mario, Luigi, and Toad, it means that for once Bowser hasn't kidnapped her! In 2013's *Super Mario 3D World*, the Sprixie Princesses are the unlucky ones to be imprisoned by Bowser.

CAT-ASTROPHE

Check out the cat theme going on! The super bell summons the feline forces and lets Mario pounce on enemies and even claw up the walls in his aim to shut down evil doings. As the battle to control the Sprixie Kingdom rages, cat scratching powers could be vital!

TOP TIP!

Need items to give you the upper hand? Dish out double trouble by cloning yourself thanks to the double cherry and stick the cannon box on your head to blast out projectiles.

TRIVIA

In 2021 Nintendo released *Super Mario 3D World* for the Switch, but also bolted on a fresh adventure, *Bowser's Fury*. Time to meet the new enemy in Fury Bowser!

MARIO PARTY

There are more than 15 games under the *Mario Party* brand since the original on the N64 in 1998. Set on interactive game boards with stacks of mini games, characters scrap to be declared the lucky winner. *Super Mario Party* (Switch 2018) added strategic dice blocks, river survival mode, and online mini games. Join the, uh...party!

GET ON BOARD

Mario Party Superstars (2021) brought back five fave boards from the 1990s, including Peach's birthday cake, Woody Woods, and Yoshi's tropical island. Mario fans also got to discover the fresh new survival course, tag match multiplayer course, and Mt. Minigames mode. Super stuff!

It's just one big party in the Mario universe!

TOP TIP!

AI players in *Mario Party* games are super lucky with their dice rolls! If you're facing them, try setting the AI players' difficulty to easy to level things up!

TRIVIA

On the same day as *Mario Party Star Rush* came out in 2016, a Nintendo amiibo figure of the ghostly character Boo was also revealed. Boo even glowed in the dark for extra spookiness!

SUPER MARIO ODYSSEY

GREATEST GAME RATING: 4

In the timeless Mario tradition, *Super Mario Odyssey* (2017) sees the naughty Bowser plan to capture Princess Peach and marry her. Obviously she's not down with this and, this time, Mario is joined by Cappy in his efforts to save her! Cappy has replaced Mario's trademark red cap and is a new character with all sorts of mega helpful powers.

CAP-TURING POWERS

Cappy has plenty of hat tricks to deploy with Mario. He offers the awesome skill to cap jump and cap throw, and Mario has the epic ability to possess enemies, items, and even T Rexes! Of course, Mario's magnificent mustache is transported to these objects while they're under his cap-tivating spell!

SECRET
If you can collect all 999 power moons you'll be rewarded with a gold balloon and a fireworks display back at Peach's Castle!

TOP TIP!
To help with challenges on the power moons, hop on a slick scooter vehicle. Scooters have a great jumping ability—super helpful when hopping over the rope 100 times in New Donk City!

It's best to keep your gaming secrets under your hat!

LUIGI'S MANSION

Hunt down the ghastly ghosts and search for Mario as Luigi enters his mega scary mansion adventure! The original *Luigi's Mansion* was in 2001 for the GameCube and the appearance of the Boo ghosts, the powerful Poltergust 3000 vacuum, and loads of exciting levels and challenges makes this Mario spinoff series a spook-tacular success!

GO GOOIGI

This time Luigi has a fiendish friend, called Gooigi! He's a gruesome green version of the title hero. He's made of slime and has the ability to slip through small spots, tread on spikes, and assist with other tricky obstacles. Gooigi looks terrifying and touching him is not pleasant but he's a grade A ghost buster!

TOP TIPS!

Using the upgraded Poltergust G-00, smash ghosts with its slam function, break defenses with suction shot, and blast groups using the burst option!

Two players can enter the Last Resort hotel levels but for an even scarier journey, take on the ScareScraper tower with as many as eight players locally or online.

MARIO KART

Put the pedal to the floor and race over to Rainbow Road for Nintendo's cool karting adventure! With more than 160 million sales around the world since the first *Super Mario Kart* on the SNES in 1992, driving fans just love revving up with Mario and his fast friends!

GREATEST GAME RATING: 3

If you want a relaxing drive and time to admire the scenery, then Mario Kart is not for you because it's action-packed all the way. *Mario Kart 8 Deluxe* (2017) saw five new Nintendo heroes—Bowser Jr., Dry Bones, King Boo, and two Inklings—join the starting lineup of 42 drivers and 48 courses to choose from. As many as eight players can connect locally for multiplayer fun and up to 12 in online races.

The racing never stops in Mario's wheel-to-wheel wonderland.

EXCITING ITEMS

As well as racing skills and bravery, items and power-ups are a major factor in all Mario Kart games. Bananas, spiny shells, bullet bills, and dash mushrooms are some of the most well known. In *Mario Kart 8 Deluxe*, Boo returned to add an invisibility function, and the feather could help you swerve attacks. This version also let racers carry two items at once—double karting chaos!

SECRET
Always be on the lookout for a secret shortcut, especially if you have a boost item to use. In Toad Harbor, use the ramps on the left by the start!

TOP TIP!

Mario Kart 8 Deluxe introduced a new smart steering option. This is really helpful for new gamers as it keeps them on track and clear of the walls. Smart steering can be switched on or off at any point in an offline race.

TOP TIP!

Try out the clever auto-accelerate feature. In the options, just select it and your motor will automatically race to its fastest speed, but make sure you can handle the acceleration and steer a safe route past opponents and obstacles!

WARIOWARE

The evil Wario has been a title character for Nintendo going back to the 1990s, with favorites like *Wario Land, Wario World,* and *Game & Wario.* The *WarioWare* series kicked off in 2003 with a minigame compilation, leading all the way to *WarioWare Gold* in 2018 and *WarioWare: Get It Together* for the Switch in 2021. These are fun games, so be a-ware of them!

MINIGAME MADNESS

WarioWare: Get It Together has more than 200 fun and wacky minigames in story mode to test your gaming skills and intelligence! The microgames really are bonkers, from pulling out a statue's armpit hair to breaking out of trash bags and assembling crazy robots. The challenges are quick and quirky and great fun when you control playable characters like Wario, 9-Volt, and Ashley.

TOP TIP!

Every playable character has a special power—Wario's strengths are dashing and hovering at great speed with his flashy jetpack!

TRIVIA

How do you reckon Wario got his name? It's actually a combination of the Japanese word for "evil" and Mario. Plus, it's pretty cool that "w" is an upside down "m"!

DONKEY KONG

The *Donkey Kong Country* games have been hugely popular across consoles and came to the 3DS with *Donkey Kong Country Returns 3D* (2013) and *Donkey Kong Country: Tropical Freeze* for the Switch (2018). That latest release sees the evil Snowmads create a deep freeze across Donkey Kong Island and the Kongs— Donkey, Diddy, Dixie, Cranky, and Funky—fight to thaw things out!

SPECIAL SKILLS

Get to know what the characters can offer in gameplay so that you can stop the icy antics of the Snowmads. Donkey Kong will hover with his barrel jet, Cranky likes to use his cane to bounce on obstacles and spikes, and Dixie unleashes a powerful ponytail-spinning move. The sight of DK riding in mine carts is also pretty special!

Time to go bananas and join the Donkey Kong madness!

TRIVIA

Funky Kong is a chilled-out dude and on the Switch's first DK game, *Tropical Freeze*, he was a playable character for the first time!

SECRET

Look out for the K-O-N-G letters secretly hidden in levels. Along with puzzle pieces, collect these to unlock extra content... or Kong-tent!

YOSHI'S ISLAND

Yoshi's Island adventures haven't seen as many releases as Donkey Kong or Luigi, but that's probably why these action-puzzle-quest games are so cherished when they do pop up. *Yoshi's New Island* (2014) pits our heroic green dino against Kamek, a magical species from the Koopa Troop, who kidnaps Baby Luigi. Yoshi and Baby Mario soon spring into action!

EGG-CELLENT SKILLS

Look out for the familiar (and funny!) sight of Yoshi grabbing enemies with his extra-long tongue and turning them into eggs to be thrown. Now, two huge eggs are in play as the metal eggdozer can roll over foes and even go underwater, and mega eggdozer smashes through scenes to rip open new areas.

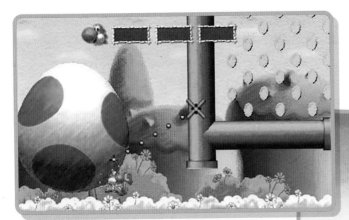

Jump on the island and get ready for Yoshi fun and adventure.

TOP TIP!

Pick up a special star and transform the hero into Super Yoshi! Super Yoshi can fly through the sky and dash along ceilings and walls. Flutter wing item also lets Yoshi soar through the sky.

ANIMAL CROSSING

If you ever thought that the cute, friendly, and addictive life-human-animal simulation game *Animal Crossing* would fade away over the last 20 years, then think again! *Animal Crossing: New Horizon* hit the Switch in 2020 and gives gamers the chance to relax and escape to an island and own a home, befriend neighbors, explore, craft, and much more. Such bliss!

NEW NOOK

Raccoon Tom Nook is one of the regular characters around the island and also a big businessman in *New Horizon*! The Nook Mileage scheme means that when you tick off certain challenges and experiences, you'll earn miles to pay off the cost of a getaway package or to exchange for rewards. Your NookPhone also has apps, a camera, and fancy filters!

TRIVIA

Nintendo is always updating the *Animal Crossing* games with online additions. One of the best is when spooky Halloween content makes a creepy entrance!

TOP TIP!

Don't worry about taking out a loan to pay for a new house. Home loans don't have a deadline or interest payments, so take the cash and splash on a nice new house!

THE LEGEND OF ZELDA

In a world of weapons, items, boss battles, and perplexing puzzles, this epic videogame series has seen sales of more than 120 million since 1986!

A brave warrior named Link remains the hero throughout this famous franchise. *The Legend of Zelda: Ocarina of Time* is a 3D Nintendo 64 fave from 1998 and later released for Wii and DS. In these versions, the master quest and boss challenge features add a new dimension as Link travels through mythical landscapes, magical temples, and dark dungeons in order to save the day and the royal family.

WILD STYLE

Link wakes from a 100-year sleep in *The Legend of Zelda: Breath of the Wild* (2017) and must explore the dangerous lands and recapture his memories. By soaring through the skies on his paraglider, riding horseback, or using a raft on the waters, Link covers the ground and scavenges for food, weapons, and items to boost his health and stats. He also needs to keep an eye on the changing weather—a lightning strike would be a big shock!

TOP TIP!

In *The Legend of Zelda: Skyward Sword HD* (2021) on Switch, players could use the new button-only controls for the first time, or swing the right Joy-Con to swipe the sword and the left to operate the shield. Bow and arrows and bombs are also easily controlled through a swish of the Joy-con!

Link is always ready to climb to new heights of adventure.

POKÉMON

From *Pokémon Scarlet* and *Violet* to *Legends: Arceus*, *Brilliant Diamond*, *Brilliant Pearl*, *Sword*, and *Shield*, it feels like there have been millions of epic Pokémon games since 1996! In 2022's *Scarlet* and *Violet*, trainers choose either Fuecoco (fire croc category), Sprigatito (grass), or Quaxly (duckling) and begin their journey through an open world where borderless towns merge with vast wilderness. Hours of fun!

HAVING A BALL

Jump into *Pokémon Legends: Arceus* and the Hisui region to begin survey missions and undertake the area's first Pokédex. You'll need an accurate aim with your Pokéball to trap wild creatures as you sneak around. The Pokéball can also create a battle if it's tossed while containing your ally Pokémon!

Look out for new releases and updates each year.

TOP TIP!

In 2020, Pokémon Home launched as a cloud-based service for Switch and mobile. It lets users switch between compatible games, trade while on the move and so much more. Keeping your entire Pokémon collection in one place is awesome!

SECRET

Look out for Nintendo's digital download special offers. In *Pokémon Legends: Arceus*, players could pick up 30 heavy balls to help catch wild Pokémon!

SPLATOON

Take cover or prepare to get splattered! *Splatoon* started out in 2015 as a four-player team faceoff and a fight to claim turf by splatting scenes with unique colored ink. It's a total art attack! *Splatoon 2* (2017) and then *Splatoon 3* (2022) took things up a gear, and in the latest title you venture through the new Splatlands as you encounter Inklings and Octolings!

FRESH FEEL

Splatoon 3 feels very familiar for fans, but there's plenty of new stuff going on to keep your finger locked on the ink trigger. Special bow-shaped weapons now sling ink and the scuttling crab tank gives teams a real edge around Splatlands. Scorch Gorge is one of the exciting new stages along with the Salmon Run co-op mode.

Get ready to paint the world in Splatoon!

TRIVIA

?

If you love colorful *Splatoon* shootouts then check out Splatfests! Splatfests are awesome online events where special characters compete. Over the years, Transformers, SpongeBob, and Teenage Mutant Ninja Turtles have made guest appearances!

TOP TIP!

Without the right gear you'll have no idea! Inkjet, sting ray, and tenta missiles were all introduced in *Splatoon 2* as new weapons—inkjet gives you fantastic flying and blaster abilities!

KIRBY AND THE FORGOTTEN LAND

Launched in 2022, Kirby takes on a new foe in the shape of the Beast Pack enemies! These nasty creatures are capturing Waddle Dees and our hero needs to rescue them from the end of each stage. You'll explore the new Waddle Dee Town, which grows when you save more Waddle Dees. Kirby's air-raising skills need to be in top gear here!

COPY THIS

Kirby's well known for his copying abilities and in *Forgotten Land* there are two new awesome powers! Deploying the drill skill, Kirby can delve into the surface and then unleash surprising underground attacks on rivals. The ranger move means that even enemies far away can't hide—Kirby's got every angle covered in this great game!

TOP TIP!

Play two player with a second gamer taking on the role of Bandana Waddle Dee. Bandana's main attack is a dangerous spear— together you'll definitely make your point against the Beast Pack!

P1

P2

SECRET

Make sure you meet up with Wise Waddle Dee in Waddle Dee Town. When you do you'll pick up some very helpful game hints.

SUPER SMASH BROS. ULTIMATE

Ever dreamed of a crazy Nintendo game where the likes of Link, Mario, Kirby, Pikachu, and Donkey Kong get involved in mega battles? Thanks to *Super Smash Bros. Ultimate* you don't need to dream! With over 70 cool fighters at launch and new heroes added all the time through DLC updates, it's a Nintendo classic full of fighting, fun, and all your fave guys, girls, and creatures!

NEW SPIRITS

Fighters can switch to become spirits and gain power-ups. The system's quite complex, but spirits can be primary or support or boost abilities such as strength and speed. Combining spirits is a top tactical move and through spirit battles, leveling up, and making a devastating mix of exciting spirits the gameplay goes to another level!

Duke it out against Nintendo's best.

TRIVIA

When Ken joined this game from the *Street Fighter* series, his look was based on *Super Street Fighter II Turbo* but his fighting style was a bit quicker.

TOP TIP!

A good move, especially for new players, is to make use of the spectator mode in *Super Smash Bros.* You can analyze player moves, techniques, and strategies to ultimately aid you in becoming the best you can!

WII SPORTS

Don't be put off by the low-key graphics and simple style—*Wii Sports* was a HUGE game when released in 2006 and is still well worth a try today! Tennis, baseball, golf, tenpin bowling, and boxing were the first activities and with the new Wii remote and nunchuk in hand, your own Mii caricature could take on as many as three friends. A runaway sporty success!

CLEVER CONTROLLER

The Wii remote gave gamers the chance to gain great control over their ball in golf, tennis, baseball, and bowling. Speed, direction, and curve could all be mastered by an accurate flick of the hand. Jumping into training mode meant spending time perfecting your sporty skills and you could even work out your fitness age through the Wii fitness test. Families and friends fought for medal honors!

There's a sport to suit every player!

TOP TIP!

Nintendo Switch Sports came out in 2022 with seven fun sports. To kick the ball in soccer, the new leg strap accessory gives you a powerful and accurate blast at the net!

JUST DANCE

Another awesome activity game originally on the Wii, *Just Dance* first got players moving and grooving back in 2009! Developed by makers Ubisoft, four players could get funky by following on-screen routines set to a variety of classic dance tracks. Over the years there have been stacks of new titles in the series to keep gamers bopping and boogying against each other!

NEW TRACKS

The tracks, dances, and artists are updated each year to keep the excitement buzzing on the dancefloor! In 2022, Camila Cabello, Taylor Swift, and Billie Eilish had new content added and through the sweat mode your exercises, routines, movement, and time spent tapping toes are all recorded to chart your partying progress!

Move, groove and get great scores.

TRIVIA

Just Dance Unlimited is an extra paid-for service where more than 700 tracks can be accessed. Seasonal themed content and grooves are also part of the offer.

SECRET

By using the *Just Dance* controller app on iOS and Android, the game fun increases as phone scoring technology kicks in for your dances!

69

STAR FOX ZERO

Jump back to 2016 when *Star Fox Zero* crash landed on the Wii U! With a feel taken straight from the incredible *Star Fox 64* on the N64, this version mixes old with new as McCloud speeds in his Arwing to lock in on Andross. Bombs, twin lasers, barrel rolls, gold rings—all the classic galaxy favorites are here for 1990s nostalgia!

FLYING FORCE

Flying master McCloud has a variety of vehicles to help grab victory in space. As well as the lethal Landmaster, check out the new dronelike Gyrowing and the Walker, which is a bipedal assault machine made from the Arwing. Using the new teleporter function you can be zoomed away to another surprise destination!

TRIVIA

Look for *Star Fox Zero: The Battle Begins* on YouTube. It's the first ever animation around Fox McCloud and the *Star Fox* team. It's out of this world!

TOP TIP!

Head into all range mode to sweat it out in a pulsating dogfight battle. You've got to be brave to boss this epic sky fight!

Enjoy space battles and master a range of machines and modes.

METROID DREAD

In another space-tastic adventure, *Metroid* came to the Switch with *Dread* in 2021 as millions of gamers visited planet ZDR and raged battle against enemies like the evil E.M.M.I. robots! Help the heroic Samus Aran in an action-packed 2D adventure where your speed, shooting, and fearless energy need to be in constant overdrive!

NEW WEAPONS

Samus has her powerful arm cannon to overpower her targets, but with new weapons available around planet ZDR, grabbing these powers and abilities is key. The beam attack can vaporize enemies and open doors and the beam can be upgraded to special shot types. Feeling confident? Play in dread mode where just one hit will wipe Samus out!

Get primed and loaded with Samus Aran!

TOP TIP!

The new phantom cloak ability in *Metroid Dread* turns Samus Aran invisible and silent—a handy tool for evading detection!

TRIVIA

? New *Metroid* fans loved getting a free download demo version of *Dread* for the Switch. It was easier than ever to step into Samus' interplanetary boots!

BIG BRAIN ACADEMY

Not every great Nintendo game has to be an all-out action quest, and the *Big Brain Academy* series gets your mind moving rather than your feet and fists! In shops for the DS in 2006, this puzzle and mental training title tests players through minigame activities in thinking, memory, computation, analysis, and identification. If you're already feeling puzzled, then your brain may not be so big!

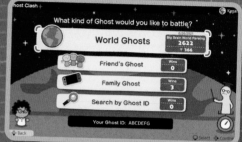

TEST TIME

In the Switch's *Big Brain Academy: Brain vs Brain* (2021), take a spin in test mode and see what Dr. Lobe awards as your Big Brain Brawn score. Keep testing and improving your score to earn in-game coins to unlock new looks for your avatar. You'll want a smart appearance to go with your (hopeful!) smart game rating!

Whack the blocks you don't need!

TOP TIPS!
Use practice mode to perfect your solo brain-training skills so you're better placed to outsmart your friends and family!

Don't bash your brain too much—set *Big Brain Academy: Brain vs Brain* at easy sprout class and then work up to the tough super elite class!

High Score

Big Brain Brawn

2544

Brain Grade

A++

Brain Type

Identify
480

Visualize
325

Memorize
798

Compute
332

Analyze
609

Your best category was Memorize!

KID ICARUS

A 1980s classic on the NES, *Kid Icarus* later hit the Game Boy Advance, DS, Wii U, and Switch online. Pit, a heroic angel with a heavy dash of world-class warrior, helps Palutena the Goddess of Light battle Medusa and her evil extras. It's a platform fantasy full of classic Nintendo styling and plenty to keep gamers coming back for over 30 years!

UPWARD ACTION

Kid Icarus: Uprising (2012) once again puts Pit and Palutena up against the dark forces of Medusa during aerial and land combats. Work out the Fiend's Cauldron, which is a complex and unique difficulty system that can reward players with superior weapons. With boss battles, multiplayer mode, and much more, it's time to master Pit and his gaming powers!

TRIVIA

?

Pit appeared as an epic playable character in *Super Smash Bros. Brawl* in 2008. Kid Icarus fans loved using his powerful Palutena's Bow weapon to smash opponents—his popularity led to *Kid Icarus: Uprising* coming out a few years later.

TOP TIP!

Kid Icarus: Uprising came with super cool augmented reality (AR) cards. Representing a character, location, enemy, or weapon, place the card in front of the camera to make it come to life in the game!

TETRIS

Line up for the greatest puzzle game in Nintendo history! *Tetris* helped the Game Boy sell millions around the world in the 1980s and '90s and is still going strong now for a new generation of puzzle-powered players.

The original *Tetris* title for the Game Boy and NES was very basic but very, very addictive to play! As the game goes on, tetromino shapes of different sizes fall down and must be arranged in a line without gaps in order for the line to be cleared. As the level increases, the blocks appear at a faster rate and the difficulty goes up a gear. Skill, patience, and practice is needed to perfect *Tetris*.

PUYO POWER

Puyo Puyo Tetris 2 (2020) and *Puyo Puyo Tetris* (2017) is a mega mashup of the popular Japanese puzzle brand and the block-beating *Tetris*. You just need to match four same-colored tetromino or Puyos characters to clear a line from your board, and at the same time garbage will be chucked into your opponent's game. What a way to "trash" your opponents!

Slot those shapes to win this block-busting game

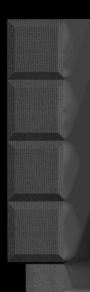

TOP TIP!
The Switch's *Tetris Effect: Connected* (2021) game has over 30 stages and more than ten levels. The zone function can stop time and the blocks falling to help you avoid the dreaded "game over" or score extra lines for bonus rewards.

SECRET
Tetris 3DS (2011) uses a clever augmented reality card to see the game come to life in AR modes and even import your own pictures!

NINTENDO: THE FUTURE?

What could Nintendo's characters and games look like in the years to come?

STREAM TEAM

Videogame streaming means sharing the games you play and the adventures you have with another audience, such as your friends and family. It's already massive and Nintendo could push the streaming tech and titles to the max one day.

CLOUD CAPABILITIES

Cloud gaming means users don't download a game onto a device - they access content through a virtual cloud system. Thousands of fun new Nintendo experiences can potentially be explored in seconds. Games could be played anywhere thanks to the power of the cloud and clever satellites, ultra-wide-band fiber or 5G connection!

WATCH OUT!

Have you heard of smart contact lenses and smart glasses? It involves information being placed right in front of your eyes and could be used to create a new-look Nintendo world with virtual floating graphics and no screens!

SWITCH IT UP?

The Nintendo Switch has stormed it for many years to become the best console ever—but will it continue? With the growth of cloud services, consoles could be a thing of the past, even with talk of next gen models under the Switch brand...

IN CONTROL

The Switch's Joy-Con is perfect for all sorts of gaming, but going hands-free is definitely the way forward! Expect Nintendo to create computer tech that relies just on user hand signals and with no handheld hardware needed. This means a gaming setup that's so smart it reacts to every move you make!

RAY TO GO

Ray tracing is a technical term to do with how light reacts in games. The more enhanced ray tracing is, the more realistic the graphics and screen style looks. Nintendo's future handheld systems will make use of ray tracing and also advancements like 4K tech instead of 1080p to make stunning screen displays.

MARIO CHAT

Over the next decade, virtual reality (VR) will expand massively to become a regular part of all gaming experiences. With this ability, Nintendo can create a platform where wearables and headsets take a player to a place that make intreracting with your favourite Nintendo stars a reality!

TRIVIA

It took Nintendo 30 years to release the mini NES Classic Edition with retro games. Perhaps in 2047 there will be a Switch Classic version—you'll be a really old gamer by then!

THE BIG NINTENDO QUIZ!

How much did you learn about gaming's greatest company? Test your knowledge here!

1. **What was the name of the real-life person who inspired Mario's name?**
   A Marty Luigo   B Mary O. Super   C Mario Segale

2. **What Nintendo console followed the Nintendo 64?**
   A Nintendo GameCube   B Nintendo GameSphere
   C Nintendo Dodecahedron

3. **What are the Nintendo Switch controllers called?**
   A Swizzle-Sticks   B Joy-Cons   C Play-Paks

4. **What's the name of Princess Peach's most loyal servant?**
   A Mush   B Toad   C Stool

5. **In the Mario games, how do you make a Boo stand still?**
   A Look at it   B Pour water on it   C Shout at it

6. **Which of these is not a princess in the Mario games?**
   A Peach   B Daisy   C Buttercup

7. **What Nintendo series has you painting walls to win?**
   A Paint Pack   B Brush Battle   C Splatoon

8. **Who is the lead character of Metroid Dread?**
   A Samus Aran   B Sandra Caplan   C Alex Allen

9. **Which of these is not a real Pokémon?**
   A Charizard   B Pikachu   C Fartoise

10. **What's the name of the flying hero based on Greek myth?**
    A Chimera Child   B Bellerophon Boy   C Kid Icarus

ANSWERS: 1. C, 2. A, 3. B, 4. B, 5. A, 6. C, 7. C, 8. A, 9. C, 10. C

SEE YA, NINTENDO FANS!

What an incredible trip through the Nintendo gaming galaxy! You've discovered all the greatest characters, games, and consoles, and picked up amazing tips, secrets, and trivia for some of the most the legendary Nintendo titles.

It's time to join Mario for another fantastic adventure! Lets-a go!